1   Land's End, *c.* 1895

2   *overleaf*   Ploughing bulbs on St Martin's

Victorian and Edwardian

CORNWALL

from old photographs

JOHN BETJEMAN & A. L. ROWSE

B. T. BATSFORD LTD.

LONDON

From '**By the Ninth Green, St Enodoc**'

Dark of primaeval pine encircles me
With distant thunder of an angry sea
While wrack and resin scent alternately
  The air I breathe.

On slate compounded before man was made
The ocean ramparts roll their light and shade
Up to Bray Hill and, leaping to invade,
  Fall back and seethe.

A million years of unrelenting tide
Have smoothed the strata of the steep cliffside:
How long ago did rock with rock collide
  To shape these hills?

J. B.

First published 1974
© Introduction & commentaries A. L. Rowse

ISBN 0 7134 2815 5

Filmset by Servis Filmsetting Ltd, Manchester
Printed in Great Britain by
Alden & Mowbray Ltd, Oxford
for the publishers B. T. Batsford Ltd
4 Fitzhardinge Street, London WIH 0AH

CONTENTS

3 Fishing boats at St Ives, which was the largest centre of the pilchard fishery. The biggest shoal ever taken was in 1851, which produced 5,600 hogsheads, or 12 millions of fish

ACKNOWLEDGMENTS

The Publishers would like to thank John Murray (Publishers) Ltd for their kind permission to reproduce extracts from Sir John Betjeman's *Summoned by Bells* and *Collected Poems*.

For permission to reproduce photographs the Publishers would like to thank the following:

Birmingham Public Library, Stone Collection (Pls. 31, 69, 102, 104, 155); Bodmin Museum (Pls. 62, 117–20, 144, 145); Bodmin Police Museum (114, 115, 129); English China Clays Group (Pls. 29, 64, 67, 83, 84, 86, 93, 96, 109, 122, 128); Mrs Mary George (Pl. 13); F. E. Gibson (Pls. 20, 46, 87, 150–54, 156–60); Mrs K. Hawke (Pl. 14); Mrs Hazel James (Pls. 23, 60, 90, 116, 125); Andrew Lanyon (Pls. 98, 140); The Marconi Company Ltd (Pls. 127, 131); Oxford Public Library (Pl. 27); Penzance Public Library (Pls. 38, 44, 48–50, 92); Royal Institution of Cornwall (Pls. 4, 9, 26, 28, 30, 33, 37, 45, 47, 52, 54–6, 58, 70–3, 75, 77, 79–81, 85, 88, 91, 99, 100, 107, 110, 111–13, 121, 123, 124, 133, 134, 138, 139, 142, 143, 146–8); Royal Library, Windsor Castle (Pl. 126); Studio St Ives Ltd (Pls. 3, 8, 15, 21, 36, 40, 51, 74, 94); Truro Public Library (Pls. 135, 137, 141); University of Reading, Museum of English Rural Life (Pls. 10, 53, 95, 97, 101, 130); D. C. Vosper Collection (Pl. 106).

4   Mid-Victorian folk at St Ives (1860)

INTRODUCTION

Everybody knows that Cornwall has a strong and individual personality of its own; perhaps not so many realise that this is true of the Cornish people too.

The little land makes an unforgettable shape on the map, jutting out into the Atlantic seventy miles long, thirty miles north to south along the Tamar frontier, narrowing to fifteen miles across in the middle, and only five from Marazion over to St Ives. (West Penwith must have been an island not long ago, geologically speaking.)

It looks like a little Italy in reverse, or at least the heel of Italy, and climatically it *is* the Italy of Great Britain; almost as warm, less cold in winter, rainier – almost anything will grow there, up to New Zealand tree-ferns, South African agapanthus, anything except (alas) bougainvillea.

Its shape is even more like the Upper Peninsula of Michigan, sticking out into Lake Superior, to which so many thousands of Cornish miners emigrated in the last century – one sees their cemeteries among the pines by the lake-shore, the water lapping up to them, and there are all their familiar names. It was one of these old folk, living their hard-bitten lives, totally uneducated, who thought that Cornwall was separated from England, only 'joined on' at Saltash Bridge.

Everybody recognises Cornwall's separateness, its *difference*. Some people say they feel different the moment they cross the Tamar (perhaps it is partly the air). An Anglo-American friend of mine settled years ago in the Far West (of Cornwall); when I asked him to stay at Oxford, he replied solemnly, 'I hope never to cross the Tamar again'. When I cross into England myself, particularly up-river over the ancient bridge at Gunnislake, I always feel like presenting my passport.

So – though Cornwall ranks as a county, with full-dress county administration from its fine modern County Hall at Truro – it is really a Little Land on its own (which is what I always call it privately to myself).

The Duchy is not at all the same thing: that means the large feudal appanage of estates, formed right back in 1336 out of the old Norman earldom, for the support of the reigning monarch's son and heir; though the Duchy owns a number of estates inside Cornwall, most of them are outside, including the Black Prince's Kennington Oval and most of Dartmoor.

Q. (Quiller-Couch), best of Cornish writers, put this charming confusion across, with his book *The Delectable Duchy*, and it stuck in people's minds.

Cornwall is dominated by the sea on every side except the Tamar; even there is the splendid estuary of the Hamoaze running up to the most perfect of our medieval houses, Cotehele of the Edgcumbes (Cotehele means the wood by the estuary). So the accent of this book is on the sea and sea-folk, fishing and fishermen and fishwives, wrecks and the heroic story of the little lifeboats.

It is not surprising that Cornwall has produced so many famous seamen, all those admirals – Sir Richard Grenville of the *Revenge*, Killigrew, Hawke and Boscawen (two of the greatest of British fighting seamen, in the Nelson class); Pellew and Captain Bligh of the *Bounty*, Borlase Warren, Sir Charles Penrose and Captain Trevenen, a brilliant young sailor who would have made history if he had not been killed early in the Russian Navy; in our time Vian and Robert Hitchens of *We Fought Them in Gunboats* – he worked out the technique and tactics of fighting them.

In earlier periods it was easier to travel by sea than across land. Turn the map round a bit and you will see that the western coasts of Europe form a unity, knit together by the sea-ways, with Cornwall at the hub of the crossings. Hence our early population, the tin-trade, contacts with the Mediterranean: our people are basically a dark Mediterranean stock. Hence too the coming and going between Ireland, Wales and Brittany – the legends

of Mark and Tristram and Iseult, Arthur and Quenevere (Jenifer to us). Hence, too, the numerous Cornish Saints crossing on their millstones. The eminent archaeologist, Ian Richmond, had a fancy that they ballasted their cork-like coracles with a millstone, into the hole of which you fixed a mast for the sail!

In the period covered by this book, the later Victorian age, it was still easier to step into a ship at Falmouth or Fowey, Penzance or Padstow or Plymouth (itself one-quarter Cornish) and sail to Quebec or New York, to Australia, South Africa or New Zealand. In a smaller way the Cornish have been quite as great an emigrating folk as the Scots, and the bulk of them are today overseas, across the world, particularly in the United States. They are to be found thickest wherever there has been mining – from South Africa to South Australia, in Michigan, Wisconsin, Colorado, Arizona, Montana, California. 'Wherever you find a hole in the ground, you will find a Cornishman at the bottom of it' – another accent of this book.

Inland Cornwall is less well known and much less appreciated, indeed apt to be over-looked for coasts and coves, cliffs and cliff-scenery. But I discern at least half-a-dozen different landscapes: the high moorlands like Bodmin Moor, a fascinating smaller Dart-moor; the farming country on the edge of the moor has its particular charm – Cardinham and Blisland, Luxulyan and St Neot. There are the wooded valleys with their luxuriant vegetation, Fowey and Fal and Looe; the happy, fertile farmlands above and between these valleys; the tormented lunar landscape of the china clay area, with abrupt and shining burrows, or the romantic desolation of old mining areas like Cheesewring or Caradon; the honest and eloquent grimness of Camborne, Redruth and industrious Hayle, the broadening plateaus of upper Tamarside, opening out to Devon; or the last secret haunts of ghost-ridden West Penwith:

Home of the silent vanished races.

ERRATUM

The hotel illustrated in picture 5 is the Atlantic Hotel and not the Headland Hotel as mentioned

5 Edwardian Newquay (1912): the beginning of its career as a resort, with Sylvanus Trevail's grand Headland Hotel upstanding, and Pentire Point beyond. The Town Beach – really *Towan*, meaning sands

These various landscapes have their appropriate occupations, in the past had a wider range for people to earn their livelihood, often the hard way, sometimes eccentrically enough. Farming comes first of all, and Cornish farming had the stability of being mixed, a little bit of everything – cattle for dairying (Cornish cream!), sheep, pigs and poultry; barley, oats and even wheat. Though not to any extent corn-growing country, the practised eye of Cobbett observed that there was good corn-growing land along the high road from Truro to St Austell, as elsewhere in mid and east Cornwall. The classic pattern that formed the mould of much of Cornish social life, and the character of our people (their individualism, for one thing), has been that of the smallholder with his few acres and cows, ready through the ages to eke out with tin-streaming, tin or copper-mining, quarrying or clay-working.

Cornish folk have always been pretty self-reliant, and from this comes their independence of spirit: their social life is naturally democratic, with an instinctive sense of equality, very little, if any, squirearchical servility. Cornishmen have also always been ready to speak up and speak out for themselves – look at the legendary Trelawny, or Bishop Colenso, or his cousin William Colenso in New Zealand, let alone professional prize-fighters like Polkinghorne, Bob Fitzsimmons, or Len Harvey in our time. With the instinctive good manners of the Celt, we are yet a pugnacious lot, especially when given offence and aroused!

Farming and mining, of various kinds, have been the chief mainstays. But this book brings home the wider spread in old days. I am old enough to remember the fish-jousters with their carts coming up to the village at Tregonissey, crying their fish in the sing-song that had descended from the lilt of the old Cornish language; the knife-grinder with the hum of his wheel and the sizzling of the blade on it; the peddlars and the gipsies with their exotic air, of whom we were mistrustful, though George Borrow, himself Cornish, made a cult of them, was adopted by them, and became their spokesman in literature. St Austell, too, had its town-crier, though not a grandee in uniform like those of boroughs such as Bodmin or Fowey, let alone the city of Truro. But we did have a relic of a more ancient profession in Johnny the Rhymer, who for a copper would make you a rhyme on the spot, often an unsuitable one (this must have been very traditional).

We see that the personality of our people – a good deal of it is reflected in the honest features of the folk in this book – is strongly individual and quite distinctive: we are no more English than the Little Land is part of England. We are closest to the Welsh of South-West Wales, of Pembroke and Cardigan (which also has its New Quay), and to Brittany – one can see this reflected in their photographs. The similarity is striking, as in the types of houses, particularly the granite cottages of Penwith, like those of Finisterre. I often think of far west Cornwall as *la Bretagne bretonnante*. These things reflect both race and way of life.

They create recognisable temperament, in which the factor of heredity is so much stronger than anything, church or chapel, class or social circumstance. One recognises the Celtic temperament in the Cornish: warm and generous, if not hurt or offended, touchy and quick, easily resentful and apt to nurse ill-feelings a long while. Anglo-Saxons be wary! for we are also secretive, reserved, mistrustful; not at all on the surface, or obvious, or so easily read as you think; very individualist and clannish, we hang together in an instinctive way, if not so good at cooperating; hospitable to foreigners – and all outsiders are 'furriners' in Cornwall – if they treat us well (you won't get much out of us if you don't); spirited and brave enough, with all the effort and struggle, the hard lot through the ages of wresting a living from a scanty soil, the perils of mining and the sea. In spite of everything, and above all, we are interesting and *different*, an individual people in our own Little Land.

A. L. R.

1 THE NORTH COAST

From **'Tregardock'**

A mist that from the moor arose
In sea-fog wraps Port Isaac bay,
The moan of warning from Trevose
Makes grimmer this October day.

Only the shore and cliffs are clear.
Gigantic slithering shelves of slate
In waiting awfulness appear
Like journalism full of hate.

On the steep path a bramble leaf
Stands motionless and wet with dew,
The grass bends down, the bracken's brown,
The grey-green gorse alone is new.

J.B.

6 The Tintagel Tennyson knew

Lovers of Cornwall, and inhabitants too, are apt to divide into addicts of the North Coast and those who favour the South. Though so few miles apart, they really are very different. The iron North Coast, with cliffs of heroic height – some of the highest cliffs in Britain, reaching to some 800 feet – faces the Atlantic: when you look west from those cliffs you are looking across to Labrador.

The Atlantic rolls in its perpetual surges on those strands, pounding at the cliffs and headlands – Bedruthan Steps, Tintagel, Trevose, Godrevy – all the way from Bude to Land's End. There is always a breeze blowing; bracing and windy, this is the coast for surf – miles of it foaming in – and surfing. Wind-blown sands and towans, the Cornish for dunes, spread down the coast, covering ancient oratories at Perranporth and Gwithian.

This is the country Tennyson visited to collect material and colour for his Arthurian poems, *Idylls of the King*. Here Hardy met his wife at St Juliot and wrote it into his novel, *A Pair of Blue Eyes* with a most exciting cliff-rescue in one chapter; after her death, he wrote those wonderful poems about Boscastle and Beeny Cliff. Matthew Arnold wrote his

'Tristram and Iseult' about it too; he was Cornish on his mother's side, but he never came. John Betjeman belongs to the North Coast school; he has celebrated the Padstow countryside in his poem, 'Trebetherick', one of the most moving to be written about a Cornish place.

Here is Newquay at the beginning of its astonishing, monstrous growth as a resort: home of the naturalist J. C. Tregarthen and of the talented family of Tangye, Quakers, ironmasters, flower-growers, writers. And so all the way down to St Ives, inspiration of admirable artists like Ben Nicolson, Barbara Hepworth, Peter Lanyon – once the centre of a great pilchard fishery, now almost submerged by the tourist industry. As Disraeli might have said, Tourism, tourism – all is tourism.

On to Land's End, confronting miles of reef – on one of which the *Torrey Canyon* stuck – fountains of sea-spray, the Scilly Isles and all the Atlantic. About this country W. H. Hudson, admirable naturalist and bird-watcher, wrote his classic *The Land's End*.

A. L. R.

7 *Above* Newquay (c. 1880) began as a little fishing harbour – here seen as it was towards the end of the nineteenth century, fishing smacks and luggers within shelter of the quay from which it took its name, the grand sweep of the bay beyond

8 *Right* Fore Street, St Ives (1910) in horse-and-cart days

9 *Left* Port Isaac Lifeboat, about 1895. *Porthissick* means 'beach of the cornfield'

10 *Below* Feast-day at Bude (*c.* 1895): a celebration on the Strand beside Bude Canal

11 *Right* Bude – early resort days: Hartland Terrace in 1895

12 *Below right* Portreath (i.e. 'beach of sand') Docks in 1898: the busy little harbour north of the Redruth-Camborne mining area, built to serve it and send ore to South Wales for smelting

13 *Left* Coronation Camp at Harlyn Bay (1911): tea-time for the George family; Gulland Rock in the background

14 *Below left* An outing of Sancreed Church Choir at Carbis Bay on 24 July 1903

15 *Below* Family Group (the Berrimans) at Treveglos (i.e. 'church farm'), Zennor, the young women wearing typical sun-bonnets

2 THE SOUTH COAST

From 'Cornish Cliffs'

Those moments, tasted once and never done,
Of long surf breaking in the mid-day sun,
A far-off blow-hole booming like a gun –

The seagulls plane and circle out of sight
Below this thirsty, thrift-encrusted height,
The veined sea-campion buds burst into white

And gorse turns tawny orange, seen beside
Pale drifts of primroses cascading wide
To where the slate falls sheer into the tide.

J.B.

The South Coast faces the Channel and looks across to Brittany: altogether less heroic and gentler than the North, it has headlands as fine and cliffs, though lower, still reaching 400 feet sheer in the Dodman, near Mevagissey. On this side river-valleys are longer, estuaries deeper and provide magnificent anchorages – Helford, Fal, Fowey, the Hamoaze at Saltash. So – sailing and yachting country, swimming not surfing, many harbours and sailing clubs, sea-salts and regattas and such.

Newlyn has its painters and potters no less than St Ives – though St Ives claims one of the world's greatest in Bernard Leach. Christopher Wood painted Mousehole and PZ

16 *Left* Cadgwith, a village near the Lizard, in 1911 – and how like Brittany

17 *Right* The Promenade at Penzance in 1896: St Mary's Regency Gothic church in the background

18 *Below* Penzance in 1908: the Promenade, looking west towards Newlyn

(Penzance) boats. Falmouth, with the deepest anchorage of all in St Just Pool, is now a leading repair-dock; Fowey the chief port for export of china-clay, directed by the benevolent octopus of E.C.L.P.

Q., first of Cornish writers – grandson of Jonathan Couch of Polperro, authority on British fishes, who wrote the standard work – wrote about Fowey: 'Troy Town' in his enchanting novels and stories. He has a successor in Daphne du Maurier, who has strayed inland as far as Jamaica Inn and as far west as Frenchman's Creek, to make them her own.

A. L. R.

19 Newlyn in 1903, looking down to the harbour on Mount's Bay

20 St Michael's Mount – Lord St Levan's boatmen in their uniform

21 Newlyn, looking uphill from the harbour

22 *Top* Mousehole – pronounced Mouzzle – as it was in 1892

23 *Below* Porthleven on Mount's Bay about 1900, fishing boats and a schooner in the little harbour, where they bring in the finest lobsters

24 Helston, Coinage-hall Street – so called from the hall where tin was 'coigned', i.e. stamped at the corner to pay royalty to the Duchy of Cornwall. An attractive, hardly changed street of local silvery granite, mainly late Georgian and early Victorian

25 Falmouth from Trefusis, looking across the Penryn creek of the river in 1890

26 King Harry Ferry, on the Fal, 1880. The King Harry referred to is the sainted King Henry VI

27 The Old Harbour at Falmouth

28 A pleasure-boat on the Fal at Feock, c. 1912

29 Charlestown Harbour, the little
china-clay harbour on St Austell Bay,
called after Charles Rashleigh who
built and developed it about 1800.
Here we see it towards 1900, crowded
with brigs and schooners to load clay,
the harbour-master's house up on the
left

30 Polperro, the 'Island', Cornish
maiden, knitting, fisherman looking on

31 Weighing fish at Polperro, in 1893: a little pilchard fishing harbour and home of Jonathan Couch, who wrote the *History of British Fishes*

33 *Overleaf* Bodinnick Ferry looking across the river to Fowey

32 *Right* Fowey in 1890: the Lugger Inn – an Elizabethan house

34   West Looe of old, looking down
to the river, 1886

35   The quay at East Looe in 1906,
looking across river to residential
West Looe beginning to spread along
the cliff

3 FISHING, WRECKS AND LIFEBOATS

From 'Trebetherick'

But when a storm was at its height,
And feathery slate was black in rain,
And tamarisks were hung with light
And golden sand was brown again,
Spring tide and blizzard would unite
And sea came flooding up the lane.

J.B.

Here we have the varied life round the sea deployed, though by no means all of it: fishing-smacks set out, bring back their catch, crabbers, limpet-pickers; fish-markets, mending nets; boatmen laying up the boat or preparing to go out.

Then there is the other side to the story — storms and fog, wrecks on the coast, the lifeboats with their gallant crews, the sea giving up her dead.

A.L.R.

36   The St Ives lifeboat putting out in rough seas, 1904

37 *Left* St Ives fishing boats – beyond, typical fishermen's houses with fish cellars beneath

38 *Below* Newlyn fish market, on Mount's Bay, 1906

39 *Right* Mending nets at Looe, 1906

40 *Below right* Harvest of the Sea – 'tucking' fish, i.e. basketing them out of the seine-net by dippers

43 *Right*   Skipper, 1880's

41 *Above*   Prussia Cove Crabbers in the 1880's

42 *Right*   Looe Fishermen, 1906

44 *Top* All's well that ends well. The American liner *Paris* went aground at Lowland Point near Coverack on 21 May 1899. The Falmouth and Porthoustock lifeboats helped to transfer passengers. After seven weeks' work the tugs successfully pulled the liner off the rocks. Here they are at it

45 *Below* Breton fishermen ashore at Newlyn, picking shellfish, *c.* 1895

46 *Right* Penzance lifeboat under sail, about 1900

47 *Below right* Padstow lifeboat being launched at Harlyn Bay, in the early 1900's, shortly after the discovery of the famous prehistoric burying ground nearby

48 All Souls Day at Gunwalloe,
commemoration of those lost at sea,
c. 1895

49 'And the sea shall cast up her
dead.' Porthleven

50 A wrecked barque at Porthleven, 1884

51 The wreck of the *Susan Elizabeth* off St Ives, 17 October 1907

52 The wreck of the Cunarder, S.S. *Malta*, 1889, with a variegated cargo of velveteen, calico, muslin, rugs, carpets, casks of palm oil. The ship came gently ashore in fog; Botallack Head in the background

4 INLAND

From 'Old Friends'

The sky widens to Cornwall. A sense of sea
  Hangs in the lichenous branches and still there's light.
The road from its tunnel of blackthorn rises free
  To a final height.

And over the west is glowing a mackerel sky
  Whose opal fleece has faded to purple pink.
In this hour of the late-lit, listening evening, why
  Do my spirits sink?

The tide is high and a sleepy Atlantic sends
  Exploring ripple on ripple down Polzeath shore,
And the gathering dark is full of the thought of friends
  I shall see no more.

J.B.

Most of the population after all, though living in sight or sound of the sea, lead landsmen's lives. The essential framework of their story is suggested by the following figures. The population in 1800 was about 190,000; in 1860 it was near 370,000. That was about the highest for the century, after the decline of copper but before the long decline of tin-mining, when scores of thousands left home for America, Australia, South Africa. In 1900 the population, in spite of natural increase, was down to about 320,000. Today – with the insane population-explosion of our time – it tops 380,000. Too many for such a small area – while half-a-million come into it in the summer!

53 *Left* Faith tea at Northcott Mouth, near Bude, 1900 – 'faith tea' meant you brought your own eatables

54 *Below* The county town, Truro: Boscawen Street, the old Red Lion in the centre, the lower part, built in 1671, the house where Samuel Foote, the dramatist, was born

All the little Cornish towns are bursting at the seams, with building development, traffic-jams and demolition for more traffic. The charming Regency area of Truro has been devastated for a ring-road. Boscawen Street has lost its historic 'Red Lion' of 1671, of so many memories and associations, its fine oak staircase, willow-pattern china, and long upstairs drawing-room of unnumbered happy social gatherings: all gone.

Cornwall does not have so much good town-building – witness Camborne and Redruth – as to be able to afford to destroy what there is.

A. L. R.

55 *Left*   Old St Mary's, the parish church of Truro, 1870; the richly carved aisle on the left, typical work of about 1500, was incorporated in the new cathedral

57 *Below*   Camborne, mining capital of West Cornwall, in 1906

56 *Below left*   Wharf and warehouses on the Truro river, J. L. Pearson's cathedral rising in the distance, one of the finest of Victorian churches. The towers of the cathedral have not yet been built, so the date is probably the late 'eighties

58 The re-opening of Great Condurrow mine, near Camborne

59 Redruth Fore Street, twin mining town with Camborne, about 1898

60 Market day at Redruth

62 *Following page* Bodmin – chemist's shop

61 The fine market-house at Helston, designed by a Bristol architect and built in the first year of Queen Victoria's reign, 1837–8. The date of the photograph is 1895

63 Bodmin Fore Street about 1901

64 Roche Church bells, after
re-casting in 1911

65 *Top* Gaffers at Stratton, 1887   **66** *Below* The building of Brunel's Saltash Bridge, 1858

67 Grampound about 1900, the little Guildhall of the old rotten borough up the hill

68   Ancient Cornish cross at No
Man's Land, near Lostwithiel, 1900

5 FARMING AND MINING

From 'Summoned by Bells'

It all is there, excitement for the eyes,
Imagined ghosts on unfrequented roads
Gated and winding up through broom and gorse
Out of the parish, on to who knows where?

J.B.

Farming speaks for itself everywhere – though it is pleasant to *see* here the ploughing with oxen at Bodrugan I had only heard about in my youth, and also from my grandfather who worked with oxen on the farm at Crinnis (meaning island or isolated round-camp) near St Austell.

Tin-mining was Cornwall's speciality – undoubtedly the Cornish had a gift, some of them a genius, for mining. 'He d'knaw tin' was the phrase, meaning practically 'he can smell out tin' – I have heard the phrase as far away as in Grass Valley, California.

Tin-miners were so proud of their prowess that, when tin-mining declined and some of them were forced to 'go to clay', they considered it a step-down. Now china-clay is the premier industry.

A.L.R.

69   Drawing water from the well, 1893

70 *Below* Bodrugan, near Mevagissey, the last place where they ploughed with oxen, 1892

71 *Right* Harvesting

72 *Below right* Croust time at harvest

73 *Below* Harvest in the Scillies, *c.* 1878 – building the pook

74 *Right* Pause in the threshing for croust, cider-barrel in the middle; about 1900

75 *Below right* Threshing

76 The end of the day – reading the Bible (note the typical Cornish range), 1909

77 Potato-crop at St Buryan, August 1900

78 *Top* The Redruth-Camborne tin-mining area, Carn Brea (i.e. Rocks Hill) with monument on the right, 1893. The picture was taken by J. C. Burrow, 'Photographer to H.R.H. The Prince of Wales'

79 *Below* A skip-shaft at Redruth in the 1860's

80 *Right* Tin miners

82 *Far right* Underhand stoping at
East Pool, 1893

81 *Below* Dressing frames at
Tolvadden, near Marazion

83 Felling a china-clay stack, 1910

84 Bal-maidens (*bal* or *wheal* means mine) scraping the blocks of clay – note sun-bonnets – about 1905

85 A china-clay pit about 1900 – pumping gear

86 Bagging the clay for shipment,
towards 1900

6 OCCUPATIONS AND LIVELIHOODS

From 'Winter Seascape'

The sea runs back against itself
With scarcely time for breaking wave
To cannonade a slatey shelf
And thunder under in a cave

Before the next can fully burst,
The headwind, blowing harder still,
Smooths it to what it was at first –
A slowly rolling water-hill.

Against the breeze the breakers haste,
Against the tide their ridges run
And all the sea's a dappled waste
Criss-crossing underneath the sun.

Far down the beach the ripples drag
Blown backward, rearing from the shore,
And wailing gull and shrieking shag
Alone can pierce the ocean roar.

J.B.

Many and various, some serious, others comic or rather eccentric. Look how serious the captain of the *Lyonnesse* looks – and how weighty! – as he grasps the rail of the companion-way to mount to the bridge. How contented the old limpet-women appear, sheltered in their cave (contrary to Trade Union, certainly sanitary, regulations). Then there's the organ-maker of St Dennis (the place not called after the Saint, but after the *dinas*, the

87 Carding wool in the Scilly Isles

prehistoric fort within which the church was built) – how clerical he looks! I'll bet he was a local preacher. And last the band – with what awe and respect we regarded the brass-band, the characteristic expression (with chapel-hymns) of the Cornish feeling for music, wherever they went.

A.L.R.

88   Fish-jouster at Penzance, about 1904

89   A St Ives Fishwife, 1903

90 *Left* Limpet-pickers at Downderry near Looe

91 *Below left* Boat-building, Mevagissey

92 *Below* Captain Tiddy, the ship's master of the *Lyonesse* (1908), sailing between Penzance and the Scillies

93 China-clay captain, Tom Yelland, in front of his clay-dry, Carloggas, 1900

94　Scalding the pig

95　The knife-grinder outside the porch of St Mary's, Launceston, c. 1900; note his sign of the shears

96   John Trudgian, the organ-builder
of St Dennis, 1889

97 Wheelwrights and blacksmiths at Stratton, 1895. Bill Woodley is in the middle of the back row; on his right is Nicholas Treleven

98 Furniture shifting at St Ives. Note 'A. Wallis, Dealer in Marine Stores' – he became famous as a primitive painter later

7 SCHOOLS, RECREATIONS, LAW AND ORDER

From **'Summoned by Bells'**

But somewhere, somewhere underneath the dunes,
Somewhere among the cairns or in the caves
The Celtic saints would come to me, the ledge
Of time we walk on, like a thin cliff-path
High in the mist, would show the precipice.

J.B.

Cornwall, being a poor county, was very backward educationally; plenty of bright-eyed, intelligent children looked up but were not fed – until the elementary schools were started in the 1870's and then the great Education Act of 1902 created a nation-wide system of secondary (grammar) schools. There had been very few in Cornwall – all was to do at the beginning of the century. And a remarkable band of public-spirited pioneers set to to accomplish it: R. G. Rows, Quiller-Couch, C. V. Thomas, F. R. Pascoe, Browning Lyne.

Nonconformists objected to Church schools benefiting from the education-rate – a great element in the Liberal victory of 1905; we see one such protester, with the fanatic look on his face.

100 Church outing at the Cheesewring near Liskeard, 1870's

Tories took their revenge by unseating gallant Tommy Agar-Robartes (killed in the first German war) – actually his family had only been characteristically hospitable and asked a few constituents to tea.

Apart from smuggling – no right-thinking Cornishman sees anything wrong in smuggling – the Cornish are an exceptionally law-abiding people. They regard those stalwart pillars of law and order, the police, with nothing but pride and familiar affection.

A. L. R.

101   Village School, Marhamchurch, 1900

102 The Teachers – Church School, Helston, May 1901

103 The children, Helston, May 1901

104 Villagers at Paul near Penzance, 1893

105 Playing Marbles at Newlyn, 1893

106 *Following page* Sunday School tea-treat at Saltash, about 1910

107 *Top* The Band – Indian Queens, 1886

108 *Below* Boys bathing at Newlyn, 1891

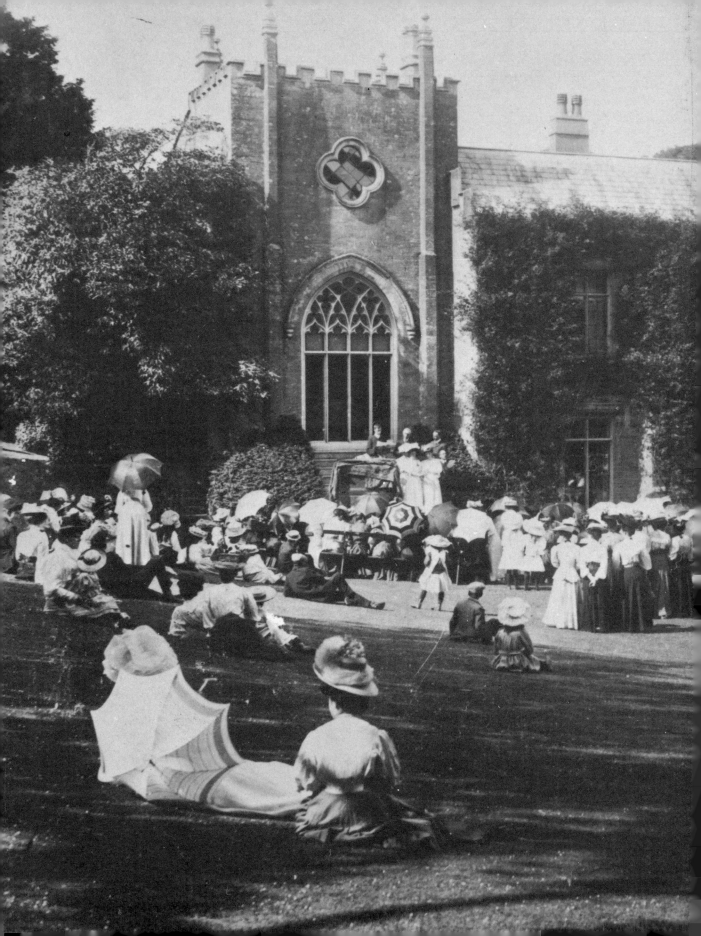

112 The Camera Club, in the Scilly
Isles

113 *Right* Truro Police Force in the
1870's

114 A Watchdog of the law – a St Ives policeman in the late 1860's

115 The First Issue of Helmets, 1889

116 Passive resisters to the Education Act on their release from Bodmin Gaol, 1 April 1905. In the middle is the Rev R. Squires; beside him C. A. Millman *(left)* and R. H. Botterell

117 *Following page* The unseating of a Liberal – Tommy Agar-Robartes, 1906

118 The Judge Has Arrived : Bodmin
Assize Hall, 1912

8 RAILWAYS AND ROYAL VISITS

From '**Summoned by Bells**'

On Wadebridge station what a breath of sea
Scented the Camel valley! Cornish air,
Soft Cornish rains, and silence after steam . . .
As out of Derry's stable came the brake
To drag us up those long, familiar hills,
Past haunted woods and oil-lit farms and on
To far Trebetherick by the sounding sea.

J.B.

Though the inventor of the steam-locomotive was a Cornishman, Richard Trevithick (we have a picture of his son, looking just like him), the creator of railways was a North Countryman, who added business enterprise to engineering genius. Trevithick first tried out his steam-locomotive at Camborne as early as 1801: this event entered into folk-memory with the popular song and its refrain, still sung:

Goin' up Camborne 'ill, comin' down,
The 'osses stood still, the wheels turned aroun',
Goin' up Camborne 'ill, comin' down . . .

But it was not until the 1850's that the Cornwall Railway began, with a line between Truro and St Austell, and not until 1859, with Brunel's last engineering feat in the Royal

119   The oldest station-master: Sam Worth joined the Bodmin–Wadebridge Railway at its opening in 1834

Albert Bridge at Saltash, that through-line connection with England was established. (Until then, we might say, England was isolated.) Scores, if not hundreds, of miles of little mineral railways existed, some of them till quite recently.

Of course there were receptions of visiting royalties on railway-stations: that of King Edward VII at St Austell is still remembered, being welcomed by an old naval acquaintance, Admiral Graves-Sawle, and responding in his strong German accent: 'Well, Sally, and whaat are you doing heerre?'

More recent and still familiar figures appear here: George V and Queen Mary, when Prince and Princess of Wales. Among the crowd to greet them in the picture – we were all sent home from school to add to the crowd – was small schoolboy, A.L.R., who still remembers it all.

A. L. R.

120   The old railway wharf at
Bodmin, the engine worked this line
from 1863 to 1893

121 The first passenger train to
Padstow, 27 March 1899

122 Bugle Station on the line to Newquay, before 1914

123 The first 'plane landing at Falmouth

124 *Following page* Arrival of the Prince and Princess of Wales, June 1909, later King George V and Queen Mary

125   Presenting Cups at the Royal
Cornwall Show in 1909

126   *Right*   The Princess of Wales
(later Queen Mary) touring the
Phoenix Mine at Cheesewring, 10 June
1909

127 Visiting the first wireless station, Poldhu. Signor Marconi following behind the Prince and Princess of Wales, 18 July 1903

128 Welcome to St Austell, 1909

129 The First Motor-Car Accident – a Cow in the Road, 1910. P. C. Pomeroy is on the right

9 CHARACTERS AND ENTERTAINMENTS

From 'North Coast Recollections'

Here Petroc landed, here I stand to-day;
The same Atlantic surges roll for me
As rolled for Parson Hawker and for him,
And spent their gathering thunder on the rocks
Crashing with pebbly backwash, burst again
And strewed the nibbled fields along the cliffs.
When low tides drain the estuary gold
Small intersecting breakers far away
Ripple about a bar of shifting sand
Where centuries ago were waving woods
Where centuries hence, there will be woods again.

J. B.

What a character Billy Bray was! He was a legend in his own lifetime – the drunken miner 'converted' and turned local preacher, jumping for joy in his newfound salvation, cutting capers and playing tricks which were re-told all over Cornwall. He became something of a folk-hero – especially to the Methodists, in a majority down among the people.

A more sedate figure, who also created a legend, was Bishop Benson, re-founder of a Cornish diocese – after some eight hundred years – and builder of Truro Cathedral. He was a creative man, a man of imagination, who found the Church in a poor way when he took over in 1877. All was to do; but in seven years he set it all going, before becoming Archbishop of Canterbury: he aroused great devotion, and never has been forgotten here.

Still more Robert Stephen Hawker, parson of Morwenstow, poet and saint, a figure to link up the Middle Ages, and the very spirit of religion, with our sad and secular days.

But there is no end to Cornish 'characters'; for one thing is clear: Cornish folk are brimful of character – like it or not, they have an extra dose of personality. You see it in the old fish-wives as well as in bishops or local preachers.

A. L. R.

A Newlyn fishwife, 'Aunt Blanche' to everybody – 1902

131 Gwennap Pit, where Wesley preached – a Methodist assembly in 1913

132 The Furry Dance, Helston, 1901

Jan said to me wan day,
'Can'ee dance the Flora?'
'Iss, I can, with a nice young man' –
'Ere we'm off to Trora

133 The Padstow Hobby Horse, 1910

134 *Right* Billy Bray (1794–1868), an early photograph of the miner who became famous as a local preacher

135 *Far right* Parson Hawker of Morwenstow, poet and saint, creator of harvest festivals in church; photographed in 1863

136 *Right* Bishop Benson, first bishop of Truro, a reviver of the Church in Cornwall and founder of the Cathedral. The photograph was taken in 1877

137 *Far right* Saintly Bishop Gott, the third Bishop of Truro (1891–1906)

138 *Right* An ancient clergyman, the Rev Edward Hoblyn, for 45 years vicar of Mylor (*c.* 1866)

139 *Far right* Trevithick's son, an an engineer like his famous father, whom he resembled

140 *Far left* A St Ives wood-carver, maker of 'Jonahs'

141 *Left* A champion wrestler, Gundry

142 *Far left* An old peddlar, Jimmy Mauld, *c.* 1880

143 *Left* A blind street-poet: Charles Paynter

144 *Far left* The Bodmin town-crier, Fred Jago, who retired in 1900

145 *Left* A street-character at Bodmin, Thomas Ellacott, in the 1880's

146 The coxswain of the Penzance lifeboat, E. Vingoe, reading a telegram of congratulations for saving the crew of the *Saluto*, wrecked in Mount's Bay, 1911

148 *Right* An old Scillonian smuggling couple: Joseph Deason and his wife

147 Early archaeology – Baring-Gould and the Rev W. Iago grubbing away at Harlyn Bay

149 Early *aficionados* of Polperro, 1893

10 THE SCILLY ISLES

From 'Trebetherick'

Then roller into roller curled
And thundered down the rocky bay,
And we were in a water-world
Of rain and blizzard, sea and spray,
And one against the other hurled
We struggled round to Greenaway.

J. B.

The Scilly Isles are an extension of Cornwall, but with a good deal of history of their own; in some ways more intensely Cornish, because of their remoteness and isolation. So that old occupations, gathering seaweed and kelp-burning, went on longer than on the mainland. Old entertainments, too – one sees why the Puritans objected so much to dancing round the maypole. In other ways not quite so Cornish, for centuries of having a garrison brought in a considerable infusion of English blood and names, fair-haired and blue-eyed strangers to mingle with the extremely dark substratum. An observant eye detects the two contrasted strains today.

Here is the traditional life of the Scillies recorded before too late – as elsewhere in this book; from the unforgettable crossing those upheaved (and upheaving) seas we all have reason to remember, to the outposted light-houses keeping their watch over the fanged reefs, the first signal to welcome the Cornishman homeward bound from America.

A. L. R.

150 Gathering seaweed – a halt in the day's work (note the old Staffordshire jug)

151 *The Lady of the Isles* in Penzance Harbour, ready for the crossing to the Scilly Isles

154 Ploughing the bulbs in at St
Martin's – St Mary's in the distance

155 *Right* Flower picking, 1893

156 Flower bunching – the family
employed

157 *Left* Dancing round the
maypole, *c.* 1875

158 *Below left* Loading flowers at
St Mary's

159 Kelp-burning

160   A visit to Round Island
Lighthouse, *c.* 1905